a Matter of Moments

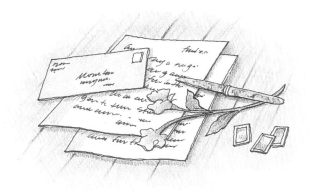

A M O N G   F R I E N D S

BY ROXIE KELLEY
ILLUSTRATIONS BY SHELLY REEVES SMITH

Published by CRACOM Corporation

12131 Dorsett Road, Maryland Heights, Missouri 63043

ISBN 0-9633555-7-0

© 1994 by Among Friends

Printed in Canada

Last digit is the print number: 9 8 7 6 5 4 3 2 1

A MATTER OF MOMENTS

*L*IFE IS A COLLECTION OF MOMENTS. For most of us, it seems those moments fly by, with so many details of our days left unattended. This book is designed to assist you in capturing a bit of time. May it cause you to reflect on the seasons and occasions of your life. Let it aid you in celebrating special dates and special people.

At the end of each monthly section, you will find space for a "journal entry" to preserve a special memory or two. Many calendars and datebooks seem to stir up feelings of guilt when not "used according to the manufacturer's directions". My desire is for you to not "serve" this book, but for this book to serve you. Enjoy—after all, life is made up of just a matter of moments… - ROXIE KELLEY

"EACH MOMENT OF THE YEAR HAS ITS OWN BEAUTY. . .
A PICTURE WHICH WAS NEVER SEEN BEFORE AND WHICH SHALL NEVER BE SEEN AGAIN."
RALPH WALDO EMERSON

JANUARY

THE BEGINNING OF A NEW YEAR SIGNIFIES A TIME WHEN MANY OF US TURN our thoughts toward the subject of "resolutions". What should be a positive beginning instead turns into a mental accounting of all manner of faults we find within ourselves. Maybe a better way to begin is with the decision to be easier on yourself and those around you for the upcoming year. "Relax" your resolutions a bit and try some of these on for size:

◆ Do at least one fun thing a day, just for the heck of it.

◆ Do something challenging at least once a day.

◆ Develop a "Six Most Important Things I'll Do Today" list. Forget about the endless number of things that could fill up pages of lists. Just six things. Do those six things well in order of importance, and you will have accomplished a great deal.

"Habit is a cable: We weave a thread of it everyday and at last we cannot break it."
— Horace Mann

To Do
1. Take a Walk
2. Smile
3. Hug a Child
4. Call a Friend
5. Smell the Flowers
6. Sing

JANUARY

1

2

3

4

5

6

7

JANUARY

8

9

10

11

12

13

14

JANUARY

15

16

17

18

19

20

21

JANUARY

22

23

24

25

26

27

28

29

30

31

MEMORABLE MOMENTS

19___

JANUARY

19___

19___

FEBRUARY

DURING FEBRUARY IT IS NATURAL FOR US TO THINK ABOUT LOVE AND romance, candy, flowers, and candlelight. I've always appreciated the timing of Valentine's Day…what better way to lift one's spirits in the heart of winter than to celebrate those we love… That's why we should expand on this tradition and include more than "mates and dates". Think about establishing some new traditions in your life every year during this heart-warming month. Here are some ideas:

♦ Remember those people in your life who have lost mates during the course of the year who will especially miss receiving a Valentine. Take time to send a card and a note to let them know they are not alone.

♦ Place a "love" note under each family member's plate, or in a lunch box, briefcase, etc. It's a tender reminder that love not only begins at home, but that it is also always waiting there for them when they return.

FEBRUARY

1

2

3

4

5

6

7

FEBRUARY

8

9

10

11

12

13

14

FEBRUARY

15

16

17

18

19

20

21

FEBRUARY

22

23

24

25

26

27

28

MEMORABLE MOMENTS

19___

19___

FEBRUARY

19___

MARCH

IF I COULD USE ONLY ONE WORD TO DESCRIBE MY EMOTIONAL STATE DURING March, it would be "anticipation". Spring teases us with a few sun-soaked days and yet we know it's too early to retire our sweaters. Almost too soon, crocus and jonquils seem to appear out of nowhere. What a source of encouragement these spring flowers are to me. Isn't it interesting how nature seems to find ways to restore our hope for brighter days just when we need it most? On one of those gray days when winter refuses to loosen its grip, why not:

◆ Send a spring bouquet to someone you love.

◆ Put more color into your life. Color has some real psychological benefits. Just a glance at a basket of five or six lemons on your kitchen table or counter top can give you a little boost. Try it!

"If you truly love nature, you will find beauty everywhere."
— Vincent Van Gogh

J. Reeves

MARCH

1

2

3

4

5

6

7

M A R C H

Mar 8/98 – Ross, Jill + Kids + Charlie come for lunch –

8

9

10

11

12

13

14

MARCH

15

16

17

18

19

20

21

MARCH

22

23

24

25

26

27

28

MARCH

29

30

31

MEMORABLE MOMENTS

19___

MARCH

19___

19___

APRIL

A SEASON OF SOAKING. THIS IS A TIME WHEN THE EARTH'S THIRST SEEMS impossible to quench. Jim Rohn, who wrote "The Art of Exceptional Living", speaks of man's need to "absorb" life's experiences more fully. He tells of a friend who had the gift of experiencing all the details of daily life so completely that it was more fun to send him on vacation and have him come back and tell you about it, than it was to go yourself. Most of us just haven't learned the art of "being there"—instead of just getting "through" the day, we need to think in terms of getting "from" the day. We are generally grieving the past or worrying about the future. This month make a point to take in your surroundings, to drink it all in, like the thirsty earth after a spring shower. Share some of those experiences with someone—the "re-telling" will etch it into your mind more deeply, making a favorite memory for you. Then take another drink of life…

"And after showers,
the smell of flowers..."
—Henry Van Dyke

A P R I L

1

2

3

4

5

6

7

APRIL

8

9

10

11

12

13

14

APRIL

15

16

17

18

19

20

21

APRIL

22

23

24

25

26

27

28

A P R I L

29

30

MEMORABLE MOMENTS

19___

APRIL

19___

19___

MAY

Having had a background in teaching, the month of May reminds me of "The Countdown". During the last few weeks of school students and teachers alike were numbering the days, impatient to get out and on with the summer. Patience is not a virtue many of us are strong in. We don't like to be inconvenienced. Generally speaking, we are a culture that does not like to be delayed, disappointed or denied. Things tend to get tense if this happens. We are accustomed to getting what we want when we want it. Patience is a quality I would like to develop in my life. Think about how patience adds a certain grace to every situation. It allows you to respond rather than react. It allows you to see "the big picture", and where you want to be, rather than where you are. A patient person is a better planner. The next time you catch yourself "counting down" or "blowing up", remember the value of practicing a little patience.

"Flowers are the sweetest things God ever made and forgot to put a soul into."
~ Henry Ward Beecher

MAY

1

2

3

4

5

6

7

MAY

8

9

10

11

12

13

14

MAY

15

16

17

18

19

20

21

M A Y

22

23

24

25

26

27

28

29

30

31

MEMORABLE MOMENTS

19___

MAY

19___

19___

JUNE

JUNE SIGNIFIES THE BEGINNING OF SUMMER, A TIME OF RELAXATION AND REST for many people. Even if our careers don't allow us a typical "summer vacation", maybe we should take this opportunity to find more ways to relax. This is especially difficult for over-achievers who are always working harder and reaching higher. But if we don't find ways to temper our intensity, we begin to fade fast. Try some of these restful techniques:

◆ Breathe deeply. It will calm you and increase your level of creativity. Take at least six or seven deep breaths several times a day.

◆ Sit in the sunshine. Turn your face to the sun and let it warm you, inside and out.

◆ Allow yourself the luxury of a Sunday afternoon nap or 30 minutes a day with a favorite book or magazine.

"But a little garden, the littler the better, is your richest chance for happiness and success."
— Reginald Farrer

JUNE

1

2

3

4

5

6

7

JUNE

8

9

10

11

12

13

14

JUNE

15

16

17

18

19

20

21

JUNE

22

23

24

25

26

27

28

29

30

MEMORABLE MOMENTS

19___

J U N E

19__

19__

JULY

FLAGS AND FIREWORKS. JULY STARTS OFF WITH A LITERAL BANG, DOESN'T IT? What better cause to celebrate than sweet freedom. Most of us realize this freedom did not come easily to us as a country, but we are so far removed from our history. In our present surroundings we tend to take our privileges for granted. From the time we are very small, most of us are taught that every privilege comes with a responsibility. Look at this list of liberties that are available to you, and determine what part you play in guarding them…
The freedom to:

◆ Choose your own set of values

◆ A good education

◆ Worship

◆ Travel

◆ Vote

◆ Peace of mind

◆ Work in your chosen field and interact with friends of your choosing.

"Countries are well cultivated, not as they are fertile but as they are free."
— Montesquieu

JULY

1

2

3

4

5

6

7

8

9

10

11

12

13

14

JULY

15

16

17

18

19

20

21

JULY

22

23

24

25

26

27

28

J U L Y

29

30

31

MEMORABLE MOMENTS

19__

JULY

19___

19___

AUGUST

IS IT MY IMAGINATION, OR DOES IT SEEM THAT STRESS SEEMS TO BE AT A PEAK level during the month of August? In spite of the fact that it happens to be one of the biggest vacation months of the year, even our vacations can turn into stressful events. Every family has one of THOSE stories about a family vacation gone haywire. No matter what the source of your stress, maybe you could benefit from some of these stress relievers:

◆ Exercise at least three times a week—choose something you enjoy. You will more likely stick with it.

◆ Eliminate negative self talk and complaining from your day. Human thoughts have a tendency to transform themselves into reality.

◆ Stay in touch with family and friends. Even if you live alone, make it a point to connect daily with someone who loves you—either by letter, phone, or a visit.

◆ Give and get hugs. Become an expert at all the creative ways to hug people (and animals!).

◆ Draw strength from quiet time and inspirational reading.

"Earth laughs
in flowers."
— Ralph Waldo Emerson

A U G U S T

1

2

3

4

5

6

7

AUGUST

8

9

10

11

12

13

14

AUGUST

15

16

17

18

19

20

21

AUGUST

22

23

24

25

26

27

28

1996- Had birthday bbp for *narm*. family- Karl & Rita & kids
Murdochs

29

30

31

MEMORABLE MOMENTS

19__

AUGUST

19___

19___

SEPTEMBER

THE MONTH OF SEPTEMBER USUALLY STIRS UP MEMORIES OF THOSE DAYS OF our youth when it was time to go "back to school". Back then it was a time of excitement—a fresh new atmosphere of learning. But the older we get, the more we allow ourselves to become anxious about new situations, fearful of "The Unknown". That's why these words, written by Robert Louis Stevenson struck a cord…

> *"As courage and intelligence are the two qualities best worth a good man's cultivation, so it is the first part of intelligence to recognize our precarious estate in life, and the first part of courage to be not at all abashed before the fact…We do not go to cowards for tender dealings…the man who has least fear for his own carcass has most time to consider others. So soon as prudence has begun to show up in the brain, like a dismal fungus, it finds its first expression in a paralysis of generous acts. The victim begins to shrink spiritually…"*

And so, I would encourage you, as I was encouraged by this wise man's words, to pursue these qualities of intelligence and courage, no matter what your age. Go "back to school" each day of your life, and open yourself up courageously to learn and share what you've learned.

SEPTEMBER

1

2

3

4

5

6

1996- Moved Norm's mom from her place in Summit Village

7

SEPTEMBER

8

9

10

1996 - Beautiful fall day - blue sky & sunny -

11

12

13

14

SEPTEMBER

15

16

17

18 Norm, Ron - raft trip until Sept 26

19 Ron's birthday - anniversary (4 yrs) of Mom's ~~death~~.

20

21

SEPTEMBER

22

23

24

Six years since mom's funeral

25

26

27

28

29

30

MEMORABLE MOMENTS

19___

SEPTEMBER

19___

19___

OCTOBER

IF NATURE COULD CHOOSE A LESSON TO TEACH US THROUGH THE MONTH OF October, it would be in the art of embracing change. So many of us are resistant to change in our lives. The unpredictable forces us to move out of comfort zone, opening us up to yet another vulnerable position in life. But the living examples set before us by nature during this month are proof that change is not only refreshing, but necessary for growth. Consider the artistry in the leaves... The ups and downs of the temperature on a warm Indian summer afternoon followed by a crisp, cold evening... The crops... Even time itself changes.

The next time change seems to force its way into your life, think of those colorful autumn leaves and welcome it, if not with open arms, at least with an open mind.

OCTOBER

1

2

3

4

5

6

1996- tried out new sewing machine

7

OCTOBER

1996 Beautiful leaves, & blue sky –
Sewed some more.

8

9

10

11

12

13

14

OCTOBER

15

16

17

18

19

20

21

O C T O B E R

22

23

24

25

26

27

28

29

30

31

MEMORABLE MOMENTS

19___

19___

19___

NOVEMBER

ONE OF THE MOST WONDERFUL THINGS ABOUT THE MONTH OF NOVEMBER IS that it hosts one of the few holidays to remain relatively free of commercialism. Thanksgiving somehow remains untouched by merchant madness— they seem to jump from Halloween to Christmas, knowing instinctively to keep their hands off this holiday that has its roots in heart and home. If we are to keep this holiday sacred, we need to remind ourselves and our children that Thanksgiving is a time to reflect on our heritage and the spirit of interdependence we share as Americans. It is a time to, again, remember God's faithfulness to us, a time to count our blessings and renew our faith. Thanksgiving is also about freedom, vigilance, discipline and sacrifice. Make it a point, this year and every year, to protect and nurture this blessed season. The power to preserve the spirit that our countrymen guarded so dearly in 1623 still rests with us today.

"Gratitude is the
memory of the heart."
— J.B. Massieu

S. Reeves

NOVEMBER

1

2

3

4

5

6

7

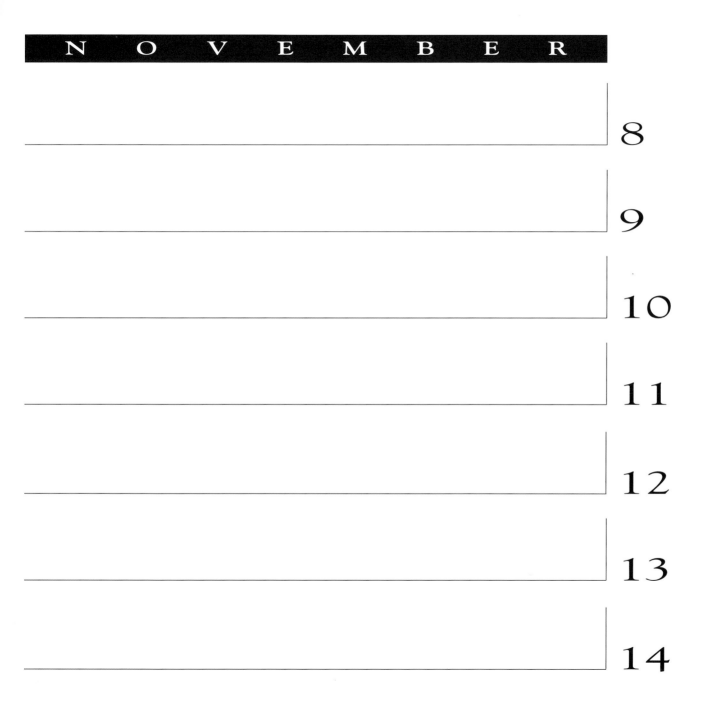

NOVEMBER

8

9

10

11

12

13

14

NOVEMBER

15

16

17

18

19

20

21

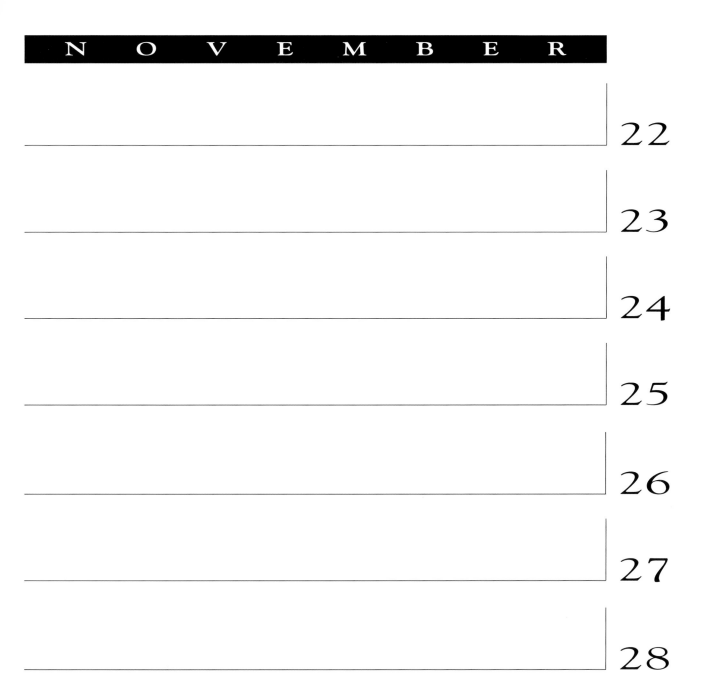

NOVEMBER

22

23

24

25

26

27

28

29

30

MEMORABLE MOMENTS

19__

NOVEMBER

19___

19___

DECEMBER

HUSTLE AND BUSTLE. LONG LINES. TRAFFIC. ISN'T IT INTERESTING HOW WE have allowed a reflective season like December to become polluted with all of this stress and mess? Most of us know we have a need for solitude and silence in our lives, but we seem to have a love-hate relationship with this. We flee from reflection, because we might recognize the need for change. However, carving out some quiet time for ourselves on a regular basis is as necessary for growth as winter is to spring. You will never hear that "still, small voice" if you don't make time for silence. And if you miss that voice, you might miss some very important messages…

Here are some ways to find some quiet spaces during December and throughout the rest of the year:

◆ Go away for a weekend alone, where no one knows you.

◆ Get up 30 minutes before anyone else does.

◆ Spread your holiday shopping out over the course of the year. Using a master list as your guide, purchase perhaps one item a month. You will enjoy being able to devote a little more thought to each person on your list.

D E C E M B E R

1991

1

2

3

4

5

6

7

DECEMBER

8

9

10

11

12

13

14

DECEMBER

15

16

17

18

19

20

21

DECEMBER

22

23

24

1996 – Xmas at home – Ron, Jill, Jennifer & Stephen, Norma's mom & Jerry – Stephen got fishing rod & helmet

25

26

1996 – cold & snowing – forcasting -40 for weekend.

27

28

DECEMBER

29

30

31

MEMORABLE MOMENTS

19___

DECEMBER

19___

19___

ADDRESSES

A D D R E S S E S

A
B

NAME

ADDRESS

CITY, STATE, ZIP

PHONE

NAME

ADDRESS

CITY, STATE, ZIP

PHONE

NAME

ADDRESS

CITY, STATE, ZIP

PHONE

NAME

ADDRESS

CITY, STATE, ZIP

PHONE

NAME

ADDRESS

CITY, STATE, ZIP

PHONE

NAME

ADDRESS

CITY, STATE, ZIP

PHONE

NAME

ADDRESS

CITY, STATE, ZIP

PHONE

NAME

ADDRESS

CITY, STATE, ZIP

PHONE

ADDRESSES

A
B

NAME

ADDRESS

CITY, STATE, ZIP

PHONE

NAME

ADDRESS

CITY, STATE, ZIP

PHONE

NAME

ADDRESS

CITY, STATE, ZIP

PHONE

NAME

ADDRESS

CITY, STATE, ZIP

PHONE

NAME

ADDRESS

CITY, STATE, ZIP

PHONE

NAME

ADDRESS

CITY, STATE, ZIP

PHONE

NAME

ADDRESS

CITY, STATE, ZIP

PHONE

NAME

ADDRESS

CITY, STATE, ZIP

PHONE

A D D R E S S E S

C D

NAME

ADDRESS

CITY, STATE, ZIP

PHONE

NAME

ADDRESS

CITY, STATE, ZIP

PHONE

NAME

ADDRESS

CITY, STATE, ZIP

PHONE

NAME

ADDRESS

CITY, STATE, ZIP

PHONE

NAME

ADDRESS

CITY, STATE, ZIP

PHONE

NAME

ADDRESS

CITY, STATE, ZIP

PHONE

NAME

ADDRESS

CITY, STATE, ZIP

PHONE

NAME

ADDRESS

CITY, STATE, ZIP

PHONE

ADDRESSES

C
D

NAME

ADDRESS

CITY, STATE, ZIP

PHONE

NAME

ADDRESS

CITY, STATE, ZIP

PHONE

NAME

ADDRESS

CITY, STATE, ZIP

PHONE

NAME

ADDRESS

CITY, STATE, ZIP

PHONE

NAME

ADDRESS

CITY, STATE, ZIP

PHONE

NAME

ADDRESS

CITY, STATE, ZIP

PHONE

NAME

ADDRESS

CITY, STATE, ZIP

PHONE

NAME

ADDRESS

CITY, STATE, ZIP

PHONE

A D D R E S S E S

E

F

NAME

ADDRESS

CITY, STATE, ZIP

PHONE

NAME

ADDRESS

CITY, STATE, ZIP

PHONE

NAME

ADDRESS

CITY, STATE, ZIP

PHONE

NAME

ADDRESS

CITY, STATE, ZIP

PHONE

NAME

ADDRESS

CITY, STATE, ZIP

PHONE

NAME

ADDRESS

CITY, STATE, ZIP

PHONE

NAME

ADDRESS

CITY, STATE, ZIP

PHONE

NAME

ADDRESS

CITY, STATE, ZIP

PHONE

A D D R E S S E S

E

F

NAME

ADDRESS

CITY, STATE, ZIP

PHONE

NAME

ADDRESS

CITY, STATE, ZIP

PHONE

NAME

ADDRESS

CITY, STATE, ZIP

PHONE

NAME

ADDRESS

CITY, STATE, ZIP

PHONE

NAME

ADDRESS

CITY, STATE, ZIP

PHONE

NAME

ADDRESS

CITY, STATE, ZIP

PHONE

NAME

ADDRESS

CITY, STATE, ZIP

PHONE

NAME

ADDRESS

CITY, STATE, ZIP

PHONE

G
H

NAME	NAME
ADDRESS	ADDRESS
CITY, STATE, ZIP	CITY, STATE, ZIP
PHONE	PHONE

NAME	NAME
ADDRESS	ADDRESS
CITY, STATE, ZIP	CITY, STATE, ZIP
PHONE	PHONE

NAME	NAME
ADDRESS	ADDRESS
CITY, STATE, ZIP	CITY, STATE, ZIP
PHONE	PHONE

NAME	NAME
ADDRESS	ADDRESS
CITY, STATE, ZIP	CITY, STATE, ZIP
PHONE	PHONE

A D D R E S S E S

G
H

NAME

ADDRESS

CITY, STATE, ZIP

PHONE

NAME

ADDRESS

CITY, STATE, ZIP

PHONE

NAME

ADDRESS

CITY, STATE, ZIP

PHONE

NAME

ADDRESS

CITY, STATE, ZIP

PHONE

NAME

ADDRESS

CITY, STATE, ZIP

PHONE

NAME

ADDRESS

CITY, STATE, ZIP

PHONE

NAME

ADDRESS

CITY, STATE, ZIP

PHONE

NAME

ADDRESS

CITY, STATE, ZIP

PHONE

ADDRESSES

I
J

NAME

ADDRESS

CITY, STATE, ZIP

PHONE

NAME

ADDRESS

CITY, STATE, ZIP

PHONE

NAME

ADDRESS

CITY, STATE, ZIP

PHONE

NAME

ADDRESS

CITY, STATE, ZIP

PHONE

NAME

ADDRESS

CITY, STATE, ZIP

PHONE

NAME

ADDRESS

CITY, STATE, ZIP

PHONE

NAME

ADDRESS

CITY, STATE, ZIP

PHONE

NAME

ADDRESS

CITY, STATE, ZIP

PHONE

A D D R E S S E S

I
J

NAME	NAME
ADDRESS	ADDRESS
CITY, STATE, ZIP	CITY, STATE, ZIP
PHONE	PHONE
NAME	NAME
ADDRESS	ADDRESS
CITY, STATE, ZIP	CITY, STATE, ZIP
PHONE	PHONE
NAME	NAME
ADDRESS	ADDRESS
CITY, STATE, ZIP	CITY, STATE, ZIP
PHONE	PHONE
NAME	NAME
ADDRESS	ADDRESS
CITY, STATE, ZIP	CITY, STATE, ZIP
PHONE	PHONE

A D D R E S S E S

K
L

NAME
....

ADDRESS
....

CITY, STATE, ZIP
....

PHONE
....

NAME
....

ADDRESS
....

CITY, STATE, ZIP
....

PHONE
....

NAME
....

ADDRESS
....

CITY, STATE, ZIP
....

PHONE
....

NAME
....

ADDRESS
....

CITY, STATE, ZIP
....

PHONE
....

NAME
....

ADDRESS
....

CITY, STATE, ZIP
....

PHONE
....

NAME
....

ADDRESS
....

CITY, STATE, ZIP
....

PHONE
....

NAME
....

ADDRESS
....

CITY, STATE, ZIP
....

PHONE
....

NAME
....

ADDRESS
....

CITY, STATE, ZIP
....

PHONE
....

A D D R E S S E S

K

L

NAME

ADDRESS

CITY, STATE, ZIP

PHONE

NAME

ADDRESS

CITY, STATE, ZIP

PHONE

NAME

ADDRESS

CITY, STATE, ZIP

PHONE

NAME

ADDRESS

CITY, STATE, ZIP

PHONE

NAME

ADDRESS

CITY, STATE, ZIP

PHONE

NAME

ADDRESS

CITY, STATE, ZIP

PHONE

NAME

ADDRESS

CITY, STATE, ZIP

PHONE

NAME

ADDRESS

CITY, STATE, ZIP

PHONE

A D D R E S S E S

M N

NAME

ADDRESS

CITY, STATE, ZIP

PHONE

NAME

ADDRESS

CITY, STATE, ZIP

PHONE

NAME

ADDRESS

CITY, STATE, ZIP

PHONE

NAME

ADDRESS

CITY, STATE, ZIP

PHONE

NAME

ADDRESS

CITY, STATE, ZIP

PHONE

NAME

ADDRESS

CITY, STATE, ZIP

PHONE

NAME

ADDRESS

CITY, STATE, ZIP

PHONE

NAME

ADDRESS

CITY, STATE, ZIP

PHONE

ADDRESSES

M
N

NAME

ADDRESS

CITY, STATE, ZIP

PHONE

NAME

ADDRESS

CITY, STATE, ZIP

PHONE

NAME

ADDRESS

CITY, STATE, ZIP

PHONE

NAME

ADDRESS

CITY, STATE, ZIP

PHONE

NAME

ADDRESS

CITY, STATE, ZIP

PHONE

NAME

ADDRESS

CITY, STATE, ZIP

PHONE

NAME

ADDRESS

CITY, STATE, ZIP

PHONE

NAME

ADDRESS

CITY, STATE, ZIP

PHONE

A D D R E S S E S

O
P
Q

NAME

ADDRESS

CITY, STATE, ZIP

PHONE

NAME

ADDRESS

CITY, STATE, ZIP

PHONE

NAME

ADDRESS

CITY, STATE, ZIP

PHONE

NAME

ADDRESS

CITY, STATE, ZIP

PHONE

NAME

ADDRESS

CITY, STATE, ZIP

PHONE

NAME

ADDRESS

CITY, STATE, ZIP

PHONE

NAME

ADDRESS

CITY, STATE, ZIP

PHONE

NAME

ADDRESS

CITY, STATE, ZIP

PHONE

A D D R E S S E S

O

P

Q

NAME

ADDRESS

CITY, STATE, ZIP

PHONE

NAME

ADDRESS

CITY, STATE, ZIP

PHONE

NAME

ADDRESS

CITY, STATE, ZIP

PHONE

NAME

ADDRESS

CITY, STATE, ZIP

PHONE

NAME

ADDRESS

CITY, STATE, ZIP

PHONE

NAME

ADDRESS

CITY, STATE, ZIP

PHONE

NAME

ADDRESS

CITY, STATE, ZIP

PHONE

NAME

ADDRESS

CITY, STATE, ZIP

PHONE

A D D R E S S E S

R

S

NAME

ADDRESS

CITY, STATE, ZIP

PHONE

NAME

ADDRESS

CITY, STATE, ZIP

PHONE

NAME

ADDRESS

CITY, STATE, ZIP

PHONE

NAME

ADDRESS

CITY, STATE, ZIP

PHONE

NAME

ADDRESS

CITY, STATE, ZIP

PHONE

NAME

ADDRESS

CITY, STATE, ZIP

PHONE

NAME

ADDRESS

CITY, STATE, ZIP

PHONE

NAME

ADDRESS

CITY, STATE, ZIP

PHONE

ADDRESSES

R

S

NAME

ADDRESS

CITY, STATE, ZIP

PHONE

NAME

ADDRESS

CITY, STATE, ZIP

PHONE

NAME

ADDRESS

CITY, STATE, ZIP

PHONE

NAME

ADDRESS

CITY, STATE, ZIP

PHONE

NAME

ADDRESS

CITY, STATE, ZIP

PHONE

NAME

ADDRESS

CITY, STATE, ZIP

PHONE

NAME

ADDRESS

CITY, STATE, ZIP

PHONE

NAME

ADDRESS

CITY, STATE, ZIP

PHONE

ADDRESSES

T
U

NAME

ADDRESS

CITY, STATE, ZIP

PHONE

NAME

ADDRESS

CITY, STATE, ZIP

PHONE

NAME

ADDRESS

CITY, STATE, ZIP

PHONE

NAME

ADDRESS

CITY, STATE, ZIP

PHONE

NAME

ADDRESS

CITY, STATE, ZIP

PHONE

NAME

ADDRESS

CITY, STATE, ZIP

PHONE

NAME

ADDRESS

CITY, STATE, ZIP

PHONE

NAME

ADDRESS

CITY, STATE, ZIP

PHONE

ADDRESSES

T
U

NAME

ADDRESS

CITY, STATE, ZIP

PHONE

NAME

ADDRESS

CITY, STATE, ZIP

PHONE

NAME

ADDRESS

CITY, STATE, ZIP

PHONE

NAME

ADDRESS

CITY, STATE, ZIP

PHONE

NAME

ADDRESS

CITY, STATE, ZIP

PHONE

NAME

ADDRESS

CITY, STATE, ZIP

PHONE

NAME

ADDRESS

CITY, STATE, ZIP

PHONE

NAME

ADDRESS

CITY, STATE, ZIP

PHONE

NAME

ADDRESS

CITY, STATE, ZIP

PHONE

NAME

ADDRESS

CITY, STATE, ZIP

PHONE

NAME

ADDRESS

CITY, STATE, ZIP

PHONE

NAME

ADDRESS

CITY, STATE, ZIP

PHONE

NAME

ADDRESS

CITY, STATE, ZIP

PHONE

NAME

ADDRESS

CITY, STATE, ZIP

PHONE

NAME

ADDRESS

CITY, STATE, ZIP

PHONE

NAME

ADDRESS

CITY, STATE, ZIP

PHONE

A D D R E S S E S

V
W

NAME

ADDRESS

CITY, STATE, ZIP

PHONE

NAME

ADDRESS

CITY, STATE, ZIP

PHONE

NAME

ADDRESS

CITY, STATE, ZIP

PHONE

NAME

ADDRESS

CITY, STATE, ZIP

PHONE

NAME

ADDRESS

CITY, STATE, ZIP

PHONE

NAME

ADDRESS

CITY, STATE, ZIP

PHONE

NAME

ADDRESS

CITY, STATE, ZIP

PHONE

NAME

ADDRESS

CITY, STATE, ZIP

PHONE

A D D R E S S E S

X Y Z

NAME

ADDRESS

CITY, STATE, ZIP

PHONE

NAME

ADDRESS

CITY, STATE, ZIP

PHONE

NAME

ADDRESS

CITY, STATE, ZIP

PHONE

NAME

ADDRESS

CITY, STATE, ZIP

PHONE

NAME

ADDRESS

CITY, STATE, ZIP

PHONE

NAME

ADDRESS

CITY, STATE, ZIP

PHONE

NAME

ADDRESS

CITY, STATE, ZIP

PHONE

NAME

ADDRESS

CITY, STATE, ZIP

PHONE

A D D R E S S E S

X
Y
Z

NAME

ADDRESS

CITY, STATE, ZIP

PHONE

NAME

ADDRESS

CITY, STATE, ZIP

PHONE

NAME

ADDRESS

CITY, STATE, ZIP

PHONE

NAME

ADDRESS

CITY, STATE, ZIP

PHONE

NAME

ADDRESS

CITY, STATE, ZIP

PHONE

NAME

ADDRESS

CITY, STATE, ZIP

PHONE

NAME

ADDRESS

CITY, STATE, ZIP

PHONE

NAME

ADDRESS

CITY, STATE, ZIP

PHONE